INTERNATIONAL LAW

UNDERSTANDING GLOBAL ISSUES

Published by Weigl Publishers Inc.
350 5th Avenue, Suite 3304, PMB 6G
New York, NY 10118-0069
www.weigl.com

Library of Congress Cataloging-in-Publication Data

Schwartzenberger, Tina, editor.
 International law / Tina Schwartzenberger.
   p. cm. -- (Understanding global issues)
 Includes index.
 ISBN 1-59036-233-0 (library binding : alk. paper) — ISBN 1-59036-507-0 (pbk.)
 1. International law. I. Title. II. Series.
 KZ3410.S348 2005
 341--dc22

                        2004007073

         Printed in the United States of America
         1 2 3 4 5 6 7 8 9 0 10 09 08 07 06

EDITOR Tina Schwartzenberger **DESIGN** Terry Paulhus

Contents

NICCOLÒ MACCHIAVELLI

Introduction

At first thought, the idea that there can be an effective body of international law seems like wishful thinking. Most lawyers would agree that, for any law to be effective, it must reflect customary practice. It should also have *opinio juris*—acceptance by the community within its **jurisdiction** that the law is binding. Many would assert that international law must also have effective mechanisms for enforcement.

Critics of international law claim it is deeply flawed, having been designed in **colonial** times by **Western nations**; that it lacks proper means of enforcement; and that, although its key institutions are still controlled by the most powerful nations, these nations do not always feel bound by the law. Critics doubt an accepted body of international law can be established among countries with widely differing customs and practices. For example, Islamic law not only binds all Muslims across the world, it states that there cannot be any other law apart from Islam. How, critics ask, can this form of law be reconciled with the precedent-based legal systems of the West? They doubt that there can be respect for international law when so many countries are ready to ignore it, or refuse to endorse it at all.

Defenders of international law, on the other hand, see it as necessary for peace among nations. International law ensures that human rights are protected, that states have universal standards to prevent

---

International law must have effective mechanisms for enforcement.

---

global **anarchy**, and that those who violate international norms of good behavior are brought to justice.

The norms and rules accepted as legally binding in relations between states are known as public international law. This is different from private international law, which regulates private relationships, such as commercial contracts, across national borders. The lines between these two bodies of law, however, have become blurred. The basic documents of international law include the Charter of the United Nations, the Universal Declaration of Human Rights, and the Geneva Conventions. The United Nations (UN) is central to international law and is charged with its promotion and development.

At the national level, states have the power to create, adapt, and enforce the law through a system of institutions such as a legislature, judiciary, and police force. At the international level, however, there is no global government. The UN remains a collection of sovereign states that are largely free to do what they like. A diffusion of power with no central authority means that, ultimately, states often act in their own national interest, disregarding the UN and international law when it suits them.

The international legal system may often be ineffective in terms of its ability to enforce decisions and, in some ways, may not be a real legal system. However, it is wrong to assume that international law is without value. It already operates across state boundaries in a fast-growing number of ways. Many people would agree that the big issues of the 21st century—war, human rights, fair trade rules, environmental degradation, and organized crime—can only be addressed through international law.

■ **Niccolò Machiavelli was an early political theorist from Florence, Italy. His theories have influenced political strategy for centuries.**

Treaties

The international community has found it practical to regulate relations between nations through a system of international rules. Agreements between nations are usually called **treaties**, protocols, acts, or conventions. Although treaties are considered more formal agreements, these terms are generally interchangeable.

Treaties regulate a number of everyday activities such as mail delivery, shipping, aviation, and technological exchange.

Increasing globalization makes it undesirable for any country to operate without the global rules defined by treaties. These

> *It is undesirable for any country to operate without global rules defined by treaties.*

contracts are the only way for states to claim compensation during international disputes.

While it may have been possible at one time to see international laws and treaties as distinct from municipal or national laws, these divisions are no longer so clear. International treaties, for example, often impact a state's domestic legal system, and national courts apply international law in their judgments.

The United Nations Treaty Collection contains nearly 50,000 treaties and a similar number of related subsequent actions, all published in more

than 1,900 volumes. About 100 new volumes are added each year—and not all treaties are registered with the UN. However, a member state cannot bring a case before the International Court of Justice (ICJ) if the treaty that has been violated is not registered with the UN. The UN, therefore, remains the main depository of international agreements.

By definition, treaties are binding only on states that agree to their terms and only when ratifications have been exchanged. States will often sign a treaty, but ratification will not come until much later, or not at all. Procedures vary by country, but in cases where a treaty must be approved by a legislature, the process can be very time consuming. For example, there are about 44 pending treaties in the U.S. Senate, the oldest of which dates to 1949.

Even when a treaty is ratified, nations will often lodge a variety of reservations, declarations, or understandings to the treaty.

There are about 44 pending treaties in the U.S. Senate, the oldest of which dates to 1949.

This means that the given state does not consider itself bound by certain articles of the treaty. Many different states use this technique. Critics claim that picking and choosing in this way often defeats the purpose of the treaty and makes universal ratification of important treaties difficult. However, it is likely that many states would be unwilling to assent to treaties if they were not permitted to make reservations.

It has become a cardinal rule of modern international law that a state's reservations cannot be incompatible with the object and purpose of the treaty. Also, in the case of a **multilateral** treaty,

■■■ **U.S. President Woodrow Wilson (right) met with world leaders in Paris prior to the 1919 signing of the Treaty of Versailles, one of the five treaties that put an end to World War I.**

an objection by one state to a reservation made by another affects the treaty relationship only between those two parties.

Over and above specific treaties, relations between states are governed by the rules of customary international law. The rules that govern treaties were codified in the Vienna Convention on the Law of Treaties. Entering into force in early 1980, the convention was largely the result of efforts of some less **developed countries**. These countries wanted to establish a more equal legal system by setting some new standards in relations between states. The convention's 80 articles were intended to put some real limitations on the freedom of states by requiring them to adhere to certain core international values, over and above national claims. By 2006, only 105 of the UN's 191 member states had ratified the Vienna Convention.

Some states have judged that the convention's provisions are likely to be applied under customary international law and have not bothered to become parties to the convention. However, the codification process created arguments over what is and what is not customary international law. In addition, some states continue to resist compulsory directives that restrict their national interests.

In May 2006, U.S. President George W. Bush and Prime Minister Manmohan Singh of India signed a nuclear power agreement. The United States Senate must ratify the treaty before it can become an official law in the United States.

KEY CONCEPTS

Customary International Law While treaties are only binding in states that agree to their terms, customary international law is considered binding in all states. Although somewhat unofficial, customary international law is based on the general practice of states. At one time, custom and treaty were sources of law that were largely interchangeable. A vast increase in the number, scope, and complexity of treaties has, however, made it necessary to define and codify the rules of customary international law that govern the making, application, and terminating of treaties.

Ratification In the United States, the president may sign any treaty that he or she considers in the country's interest. The Constitution dictates that the senate must approve a treaty before the president can ratify it. The president may, however, sign and ratify, or conclude, executive agreements in certain defined cases. Executive agreements are agreements between a U.S. president and a foreign head of state that have not been given approval by the senate. These agreements have the status of full treaties in international law. The Australian constitution, in direct contrast, gives parliament no formal role in treaty making. In Australia, this is the exclusive privilege of the prime minister.

Vienna Convention on the Law of Treaties The convention was adopted on May 22, 1969, and opened for signature on May 23, 1969, by the United Nations conference on the Law of Treaties. The convention organized the existing customary international law on treaties, filled in some gaps, and made a number of clarifications.

Born: December 28, 1856, in Staunton, Virginia

Died: February 3, 1924

Education: Law degree from the University of Virginia and a Ph.D. in History from Johns Hopkins University

Legacy: His strong belief in international cooperation through an association of nations led to the creation of the League of Nations, and ultimately the United Nations.

Navigate to **www.white house.gov/history/ presidents/ww28.html** for more information about Woodrow Wilson. Also search for "League of Nations" on **www.encarta.com** to learn more about Woodrow Wilson's legacy.

People in Focus

Woodrow Wilson was the 28th president of the United States. He served two terms as president, from 1913–1921. Following World War I, Wilson dreamed of international cooperation through an association of nations. This led to the creation of the League of Nations, and ultimately the United Nations. For his efforts in creating the League of Nations, Wilson was awarded the 1919 Nobel Peace Prize.

In 1873, Wilson attended Davidson College in North Carolina. The following year he enrolled at the College of New Jersey, which later became Princeton University. Wilson entered law school at the University of Virginia and received his law degree in 1882.

Unhappy in the legal profession, Wilson entered graduate school at Johns Hopkins University and earned a Ph.D. in History. Wilson worked as a professor at various universities until the College of New Jersey offered him a professorship, which he accepted in 1890.

In 1910, Wilson left his job as professor at Princeton to begin his career in politics. After serving as the governor of New Jersey, he ran for president in 1912. Wilson increased American participation in world affairs more than any other president.

Western Roots

More than 2,300 years ago, the philosopher Aristotle advanced the idea that there is a system of justice derived from nature that is common to all humanity. Eventually becoming known as natural law, this concept served as the intellectual foundation for much of western culture. For some nations in other parts of the world, international law remains too influenced by its Western roots.

International law developed among the early **nation-states** of Europe. It was not until the fifteenth century that the concept of international law would even begin to make sense.

In fact, the concept of territorial sovereignty of nation states was only formalized in

---

As Western powers expanded their colonial empires, they largely controlled international law.

1648 when the treaty of the Peace of Westphalia was signed. Of course, diplomatic relations between communities had existed for centuries, but defining the relations between sovereign countries with defined boundaries was new. The Peace of Westphalia represented a turning point in the conceptualization of the international community.

For 250 years after the Peace of Westphalia, the international community was narrowly defined. A European congress was called to reestablish Europe's territorial divisions after Napoleon's downfall. The 1815 Congress of Vienna further clarified relationships between

■■■■ The Treaty of Münster, which recognized the Dutch Republic as a sovereign state, was signed as part of the Peace of Westphalia. Bartholomeus van der Helst painted *The Militia Banquet* to celebrate the occasion.

The League of Nations Council met every year in January, May, and September.

European powers, but it did not involve countries outside of Europe.

As Western powers expanded their colonial empires, they largely controlled international law. A Western legal regime serving the interests of the colonizers and their nationals living abroad dominated. Attempts to restrain European control of international law were marginal.

International law did not become truly international until after World War I. The war drew countries outside of Europe into the conflict. Its devastation created a desire for a more durable peace. Initiated largely by U.S. President Woodrow Wilson, a covenant for the League of Nations was drawn up, establishing mechanisms for the arbitration of international disputes. The covenant was ratified in early 1920 by more than 40 states, 26 of which were non-European. The preamble to the covenant called on its members to accept "obligations not to resort to war." Achieving international peace required

---

Several big powers failed to support the League of Nations.

"the firm establishment of the understandings of international law as the actual rule of conduct among Governments."

The league's covenant was a landmark document because it attempted to institutionalize a set of rules for a community of nations beyond Europe. Unfortunately, several big powers failed to support the League of Nations. Germany was a member for only 7 years, beginning in 1926. The Union of Soviet Socialist Republics (USSR) was a member for 5 years, beginning in 1934. Japan and Italy both withdrew their membership in the 1930s. American diplomats encouraged the league's activities and attended meetings unofficially, but the United States never joined. The league depended mainly on Great Britain and France, who were understandably reluctant to act forcefully. It was difficult for governments long accustomed to operating independently to work through the new organization.

Although the organization ultimately collapsed with the onset of World War II, the league experienced some initial success in dispute resolution.

Overall, there was a lack of political will to enforce sanctions on states with goals of expansion, notably Germany, Italy, and Japan. In the meantime, the league's Permanent Court of International Justice established a body of **case law** based on the arbitration of disputes between countries, thus codifying some of the standards of an evolving international legal regime.

While the United Nations' architects endeavored to avoid the pitfalls of the League of Nations, the new UN charter still adhered to a doctrine of national sovereignty. This is important from a legal point of view because the UN charter is considered a primary document of international law. The major European powers were disinclined to give the new body any real independence and sought to maintain their own prerogatives. Foremost among these was ensuring that the power politics of the post-World

---

The UN charter is considered one of the primary documents of international law.

War II environment became enshrined in law in the charter. Thus, five of the victors—the United States, Great Britain, Union of the Socialist Soviet Republics, China, and France— gave themselves permanent seats on the **Security Council** and a **veto** power over any decisions about war and peace. With such power, the "Big Five" could also prevent the imposition of sanctions on themselves for transgressions of the charter in a way other states could not.

This fact alone points to a fundamental flaw in the international legal regime. While these political inequalities may be legal according to the UN charter, whether they are just or ethical is open to debate. Since World War II, developing countries with large populations, such as India, Brazil, and Nigeria, have argued that, in the interests of fairness and democracy, they deserve more power in the Security Council. However, attempts to ensure that the council is more

The United Nations Security Council studies matters of international law and security including chemical arms and criminal tribunals.

representative have been largely unsuccessful.

These political imbalances and the onset of the **Cold War** ultimately created divisions within the UN between the Western powers and developing countries. The ideologies, or political philosophies, of Western countries were markedly different from those of developing countries. Western nations wanted to maintain the status quo and ensure legal changes did not run counter to national interests. Developing countries were primarily interested in a socialist mandate and more equal economic opportunities. Developing countries were more concerned about the big powers meddling in their affairs, as well as with greater economic and social rights.

The Group of 77 (G-77) was established on June 15, 1964, by 77 developing countries from Africa, Asia, and Latin America. The G-77 is the largest Third World coalition in the United Nations. It now includes 132 countries. The group provides a vehicle for the developing world to articulate and promote its collective economic interests. It

---

Those outside the Western sphere of influence are determined to have their say.

---

enhances the member countries' negotiating power in all major international economic issues in the UN system, and it promotes economic and technical cooperation among developing countries. The G-77 ultimately holds a majority in the UN's General Assembly and pushes for a variety of new legal instruments dealing with human rights and global management. Those outside the Western sphere of influence are determined to have their say.

Despite this polarization in the UN during the first several decades of its existence, the end of the Cold War meant less pressure to align with either the United States and its allies or the communist countries. Developing countries also realized that alienating Western powers was not always in their best interest. Hence, from the 1990s, there has been more willingness to work together in coalitions and to negotiate texts of treaties by consensus. Ultimately, despite the representation of 191 states at the UN, the reality is that some members have more political power than others, significantly affecting their interpretation of international law.

KEY CONCEPTS

Natural Law Natural law is a set of principles that are based on assumed permanent characteristics of human nature that can serve as a standard for evaluating conduct and civil laws. Natural law is considered fundamentally unchanging and universally applicable.

Developing Countries Also called the Third World, these countries are economically and technologically less developed than the industrialized world. Developing countries are generally very poor and rely on aid and assistance from developed countries.

General Assembly When the countries of the UN meet as a group, they are called the General Assembly. The assembly sets the agenda for UN operations, but it has no law-making power. Each country has the chance to speak and be heard on any matter in the General Assembly.

The Peace of Westphalia The Thirty Years' War was a series of European conflicts lasting from 1618 to 1648. The conflicts involved most western European countries and was fought mainly in Germany. On October 24, 1648, the Peace of Westphalia was signed in Münster, Germany. The treaty established Switzerland and the Dutch Republic (the Netherlands) as independent states, ensured France would emerge as the chief power on the European mainland, and delayed Germany's political unification.

The International Court of Justice

The International Court of Justice (ICJ), based in The Hague, Netherlands, was inaugurated on April 18, 1946. As the principal judicial organ of the UN, the ICJ has two roles — to settle legal disputes submitted by states in accordance with international law and to give advisory opinions on legal questions referred to it by authorized international organizations and agencies.

The ICJ only makes legal decisions based on the principles agreed to by the world's nations. However, fewer than one-third of the UN's member countries have accepted the court's authority. Egypt, India, Japan, Nigeria, and Great Britain are among the countries that have accepted the ICJ. Countries that have been unwilling to accept the ICJ's authority include China, France, Russia, and the United States. Other countries accept the court's authority only on some matters.

Every three years, elections are held for five of the 15 seats in the court. The UN General Assembly and the Security Council, sitting independently of each other, elect each judge to a nine-year term. Each judge in the court must be a citizen of a different country. Retiring judges may be re-elected. The members of the court do not represent their governments. They are independent magistrates. Judges must be qualified for appointment to the highest judicial offices in their countries or be jurists, or legal experts, of recognized

■■■■ There are no appeals in the International Court of Justice. However, in the case of further dispute, the Security Council may become involved.

The International Court of Justice operates out of the Peace Palace in The Hague, Netherlands.

competence in international law. The world's principal legal systems and the main forms of civilization must be reflected in the court's composition.

Since its creation in 1946, the court has delivered 92 judgments and given 25 advisory opinions. The cases heard by the court over this time have added to an evolving body of international law. Nonetheless, with a lack of compulsory jurisdiction, the court is also severely handicapped. States decide which cases they will submit to the court. When major conflicts arise, disputed states are more often brought to political forums such as the Security Council rather than to an impartial jury. Such behavior represents a fundamental lack of trust

---

Thus far, nations have complied with nearly every final decision.

---

in the institution, especially considering no new cases were brought before the court between 1962 and 1971. In the early 1970s, the UN General Assembly made a special effort to focus on the court's role. Since then, the number of major cases heard has increased substantially, among them cases arising from conflicts in Bosnia and Kosovo, and the Lockerbie bombing.

Once a state decides to bring a case before the court, it is bound to accept and implement the court's decision. While the court itself has no means for enforcement, international pressure has often been effective. Thus far, nations have complied with nearly every final decision. There is no other judicial body in the world that has the same ability to deal with problems in the international community. In doing so, the ICJ offers states a wide range of opportunities for promoting the rule of law.

Does Might Make Right?

Before the end of the 19th century, states did not tolerate restrictions on what they considered to be their sovereign right to wage war. The first attempts to set limitations on some kinds of warfare came in the mid-19th century, with international negotiations on how to treat the wounded in times of war occurring in 1864. Initiated by the founder of the Red Cross, Swiss philanthropist Jean Henri Dunant, the results of these negotiations became known as the Geneva Conventions. The Hague Convention in 1899 also adopted some general customs of war on land and at sea. The League of Nations Covenant, ratified in 1920, after World War I. The covenant established a customary norm, making it inappropriate for a state to wage war except under exceptional circumstances.

Still, tensions remained between those states still committed to military power as the basis of international politics and others looking for a new legal framework to bind the actions of member states. These tensions were

■■■ **During the Soviet-Afghan War, Afghan rebels combated Soviet air power with the use of shoulder-fired antiaircraft missiles supplied by the United States.**

best illustrated when, about a month after the charter of the United Nations was signed in San Francisco, the first atomic bomb was dropped on Hiroshima. While the international community desired a system "to save succeeding generations from the scourge of war," it had also been made clear that those with the most destructive weapons still had great influence.

About a month after the charter of the United Nations was signed, the first atomic bomb was dropped on Hiroshima.

Nonetheless, the horrific consequences of World War II did change thinking about when it was, and was not, appropriate for a state to use force. In essence, the United Nations Charter made such acts of aggression, including the "threat or use of force against the territorial integrity or political independence of any state" (Article 2) an international crime. However, given that national sovereignty remained a founding principle of the United Nations Charter, it was still possible for member states to act in self-defense. "Nothing

in the present charter shall impair the inherent right of individual or collective self-defense if an armed attack occurs against a Member of the United Nations" (Article 51). Since the drafting of the charter, the precise definition of this article has been the subject of a great deal of legal interpretation and debate.

According to international law, resorting to force for self-defense is only permissible when repelling an armed attack. In practice, however, Article 51 has been invoked on several occasions when the claim of self-defense was widely disputed. The article was invoked during the USSR's interventions in Hungary in 1956 and Afghanistan in 1979, Israel's attack on Egypt in 1967 and Iraq in 1981, and South Africa's incursions into neighboring states in the late 1970s. Debate continues over the legality of the use of force by one state against another in cases of armed infiltration or when the lives of one's nationals residing in another country are threatened.

Among the most controversial topics in recent decades has been the legality of anticipatory self-defense, or making a preemptive strike against another state that is believed to be an imminent threat.

■■■ **At the United Nations, U.S. Secretary of State Colin Powell made the case for the United States to invade Iraq in 2003.**

In 1975, when Israel attacked Palestinian camps in Lebanon, claiming that its action was preventive and not punitive, it was widely condemned by the international community. Lebanon's UN delegate noted that, if states were allowed to determine on their own what should be termed preventive acts, the world would be led back to the "law of the jungle." In practice, various states have supported the concept of anticipatory defense in UN deliberations, depending on when it suits them, while others have refuted this doctrine entirely.

In addition to permitting the use of force by an individual state for purposes of self-defense, the UN charter also allows for collective enforcement action. These guidelines are defined by Chapter VII of the UN charter, which gives the Security Council a legal basis to authorize a collective response to threats to peace. In practice, the collective security system originally envisioned by the UN charter—with an on-call army and a UN Military Staff Committee—never materialized, due, in part, to the onset of the Cold War.

What emerged instead were UN peacekeeping missions. These mandates were generally limited to policing a territory at a state's request. Although having some success with monitoring border disputes, among other tasks, these missions were largely based on a principle of neutrality, and with a few exceptions, such as the UN

Various states have supported the concept of anticipatory defense in UN deliberations.

Congo Operation (ONUC) in 1960, these missions were not given the authority or means to conduct operations that involved any use of force. For the most part, UN peacekeeping operations have tended to be **ad hoc** and beset with financial problems.

To fill in some of these gaps, a leading power or regional organization will sometimes be appointed to carry out enforcement action. The North Atlantic Treaty Organization (NATO) was authorized to ensure implementation of the Dayton Accords to end hostilities in the former Yugoslavia in Bosnia-Herzegovina during the mid-1990s. However, while deputization may get the job done, it does point to a fundamental problem with the present international system —there is no real mechanism in place to take enforcement action on behalf of the international community.

The U.S.-led invasion of Iraq in 2003 generated fierce legal debate. The United States and Great Britain claimed that Iraq posed an imminent threat to their national security. Security Council Resolutions 678 and 687, passed during and after the Gulf War in 1991, required Iraq disarm and account for its arsenal of **weapons of mass destruction** and authorized the use of all necessary means to enforce compliance. Resolution 1441, passed by the UN Security Council in November 2002, found Iraq in material breach of its obligations.

The majority of experts in international law, although by no means all, disagreed. Resolution 1441, they said, did not authorize war against Iraq. It only required Iraq to cooperate with the UN's inspection regime. The words "all necessary means" had been deliberately left vague so that a further resolution was needed before any military action could be taken against Iraq. They also claimed that there was no proof of Iraq's continued possession of weapons of mass destruction, nor of its involvement in the terrorism against which the United States claimed to be defending itself.

In the UN Security Council, France and Russia, both with veto power, together with Germany and some non-aligned members, refused to support a second resolution sought by the United States and Great Britain. This resolution intended to legitimize the military action for which they had by then already prepared. When the United States and its partners opted to act unilaterally, they faced a wall of criticism, not just from other governments, but also from public opinion worldwide.

In reality then, powerful states may still be able to act on their own, but the failure to achieve international legitimacy has raised major legal and ethical issues. It has also exposed the weaknesses of the present system of international law and order.

WHAT IS A JUST WAR?

The concept of "just war" is as old as warfare and was first developed by early Christian thinkers. St Augustine said the only just cause for a war is the desire for peace, and that it must be fought under a lawful authority. Both of these ideas eventually found their way into both the charter for the Nuremberg war crimes trials and the UN Charter. While war is terrible , it is sometimes necessary.

While critics hold that moral standards have no place in warfare, the international community has largely accepted that there are key factors to consider when determining if force is justified. A war may be considered just if it is used as a last resort, has a just cause, is declared by a legitimate authority, has the right intention, and has a reasonable chance of success. Once a decision has been made to go to war, further considerations are made concerning its conduct. These might include determining if the end is proportionate to the means and if discriminations are being made between combatants and civilians

These principles have been severely tested in recent years. For example, is replacing a tyrannical regime a just cause for war? If the majority of citizens in a democracy oppose war against the policy of their elected government, which is the legitimate authority? Is it right to acquiesce to **genocide** when the costs of resisting it are exorbitant? Should civilians in the vicinity of a military target be considered "collateral damage"? Do weapons of mass destruction make the concept of just war irrelevant? In the pluralist context of international law, these questions are not easy to answer.

In 1998, a border dispute caused conflict in Ethiopia and Eritrea. Though the countries reached an agreement in 1999, fighting began again in 2000. The United Nations Mission in Ethiopia and Eritrea (UNMEE) peacekeeping mission was first deployed after a cease-fire agreement was signed later that year.

KEY CONCEPTS

Geneva Conventions The Geneva Conventions are a series of international agreements that developed humanitarian law intended to protect wounded combatants and civilians during times of war or other conflicts. There have been four Geneva Conventions, each subsequently amended. The first convention, adopted in 1864, provided for the protection of sick and wounded soldiers on the battlefield. The second convention, formulated in 1868, extended those protections to sailors wounded in sea battles. The third convention, in 1929, protected prisoners of war. It legislated that prisoners of war were not criminals and should be treated humanely and released at the end of hostilities. The fourth convention, ratified in 1949, rewrote, expanded, and replaced the language of the first three conventions. It also called for the protection of civilians during wartime, bringing civilians under the protection of international laws that prohibit murder, torture, hostage-taking, and extra-judicial sentencing and executions.

Peacekeeping Peacekeeping is a form of military action whereby special forces are sent to a region to preserve the peace and prevent previously warring sides from starting to fight again. The troops for these missions are drawn from the armed forces of UN member nations. Some of the many duties of peacekeeping forces include acting as buffers between warring forces, destroying surrendered weapons, monitoring ceasefires, and providing humanitarian aid.

UN Charter The UN charter was signed on June 26, 1945, in San Francisco, and came into effect on October 24, 1945. The charter outlines the purposes of the UN — to maintain international peace and security; to develop friendly relations among states; and to achieve cooperation in solving international economic, social, cultural, and humanitarian problems. The document is made up of a preamble and 19 chapters, which are divided into 111 articles.

Born: October 11, 1884, in New York City

Died: November 7, 1962

Legacy: United States representative to the United Nations, Chair of the UN Human Rights Commission, played a critical role in the writing and adoption of the Universal Declaration of Human Rights

For more information on Eleanor Roosevelt and President Franklin D. Roosevelt, click on **www.feri.org**. Visit **www.whitehouse. gov/history/firstladies/ ar32.html** to learn more about Eleanor's work as first lady.

People in Focus

Eleanor Roosevelt was first lady to the 32nd president of the United States, Franklin Delano Roosevelt. Eleanor had an active political and public career of her own, and she maintained a high profile throughout her life. She was a lifelong leader on social issues and has come to be known as the "First Lady of the World."

When Franklin Roosevelt was elected president in 1932, Eleanor was an independent journalist who spoke out on controversial issues. She responded to the problems, needs, and views of her readers in her monthly magazine column. While her husband was in office, she lobbied for greater relief for women and special programs for the youth of the country. She also was a strong advocate for African American rights, and in 1935, she became the first resident of European ancestry in Washington, DC, to join the National Association for the Advancement of Colored People (NAACP), the nation's most important civil rights organization.

Eleanor is remembered for her work with the United Nations. In 1945, she accepted an appointment from President Henry S. Truman, Franklin Roosevelt's successor, to serve as U.S. representative to the United Nations. From 1946 to 1951, she was chair of the UN Human Rights Commission. Under her leadership, the Universal Declaration of Human Rights was written and unanimously adopted in 1948 by the Human Rights Commission. The declaration has endured as a universally accepted standard of achievement for all nations.

Crimes Against Humanity

Recent initiatives to prosecute individuals accused of genocide have their roots in the Nuremberg War Crimes **Tribunal**, which took place after World War II. Some criticized the trials because, in essence, the winning powers—the United States, Great Britain, the USSR, and France—took on the role of judge and prosecutor. Regardless, the Nuremberg trials set a precedent in international law. For the first time, individuals, not just states, could be held accountable for atrocities committed during times of war.

The Nuremberg trials preceded the establishment of the UN Genocide Convention in 1948. This act, which took effect in 1951, provided a legal definition of genocide and established it as a crime under international law. According to the convention, any of the following actions, when committed with the intent to eliminate a particular national, ethnic, racial, or religious group, constitutes genocide: killing members of the group, causing serious bodily or mental harm to members of the group, deliberately inflicting conditions of life calculated to kill the group, imposing measures intended to prevent births

The Nuremberg trials set a precedent in international law.

within the group, and forcibly transferring children out of the group.

The idea of prosecuting war crimes at a permanent international criminal court was often contemplated between 1950–2000, but political realities made it impractical. During the Cold War, most knew that international prosecutions would have been used for little more than propaganda purposes.

Some of the most horrendous crimes against humanity to escape prosecution were those of Pol Pot in the late 1970s. Pol Pot was the minister of Cambodia from 1976 to 1979 and the leader of the Khmer Rouge political movement . Despite causing the deaths of an estimated one million people from forced labor, starvation, disease, torture, or execution,

■ In total, there were 13 Nuremberg war trials. The International Military Tribunal was the first trial and dealt with major Nazi government officials.

■■■■ Some of the prisoners believed to have taken part in the 1994 Rwanda genocide must attend solidarity camps in Rwanda. These camps seek to bridge cultural gaps.

Pol Pot was never brought to account for his crimes and died a natural death in 1998.

The Cold War was barely over when the brutality of events in the former Yugoslavia in the early 1990s emerged. The humanitarian crimes committed included **ethnic cleansing**, mass graves, forced transfer of populations, systematic rape, and detention camps. These crimes were large enough in scale to revive the concept of war crimes prosecutions. With more than 250,000 people killed and 1 million displaced, public pressure called for justice. Although those committing these crimes saw initial UN Security Council warnings as empty threats, the council established the International Criminal Tribunal for the Former Yugoslavia (ICTY) on May 25, 1993.

The ICTY aimed to prosecute people "responsible for serious violations of international humanitarian law committed in the territory of the former Yugoslavia since 1991." It was the first ad hoc, nonmilitary, international criminal tribunal. While initially only managing to bring lower level officials to trial, the tribunal eventually focused on those at higher levels of authority. The biggest catch

> ## War crimes committed in civil wars, not just international ones, were now subject to prosecution.

was the **indictment** of a sitting head of state, Slobodan Milosevic, on war crimes charges in May 1999. Violations of the laws or customs of war in Bosnia and Croatia were added a year and a half after that. He was forced to resign and a year later extradited to stand trial in the The Hague. Slobodan died

before its conclusion after five years in prison. From a legal point of view, the ICTY established the principle that war crimes committed in civil wars, not just international wars, were now subject to prosecution.

The tragedies in Yugoslavia are just one example of such brutality. In Rwanda in the spring of 1994, the Hutu majority slaughtered 500,000 to 1 million of their neighbors, predominantly Tutsi, in 10 weeks. Acting more quickly this time, the UN Security Council set up an International Criminal Tribunal for Rwanda (ICTR) within the year. In the meantime, there was much diplomatic soul searching about why action was not taken sooner to avert the tragedy from occurring.

Both tribunals were an advance over Nuremberg. The accused were not those who had lost a war, and the tribunals were able to base indictments on a more substantial body of law.

Nonetheless, the temporary tribunals for both Yugoslavia and Rwanda have also drawn significant criticism. Besides difficulties apprehending the accused, the tribunals—especially in Rwanda—have been criticized for extensive delays, ineffectiveness, bias in favor of NATO countries, and lack of due process, or the entitlement of citizens to proper legal procedures. It is also very costly. The two-year budget for the tribunal for 2004 and 2005 was $271,854,600, borne by all UN members. However, the tribunals have not been known for dispensing justice quickly.

In October 2002, despite 112 indictments being handed down in Yugoslavia and 80 in Rwanda, only five people were serving sentences for crimes committed in the former Yugoslavia and eight for crimes committed in Rwanda. Many others are involved in proceedings or await trial. Of course, without active steps being taken by the UN's member states to arrest suspects, many of the guilty will remain free. In one example, former Bosnian Serb military chief Ratko Mladic, although indicted by the ICTY, enjoyed ski outings within sight of NATO forces who did not have the authority to arrest him. Romanian government and Serbian sources claimed that on February 22, 2006, Mladic was arrested in Romania by a joint Romanian-British special operation carried out by troops of those respective countries.

■■■ **General Ratko Mladic was accused of crimes against humanity for his role in the ethnic cleansing of Yugoslavia.**

However, Chief UN Prosecutor Carla del Ponte denied the rumors that Mladic had been

The tribunals have not been known for dispensing justice quickly.

arrested, claiming they had "absolutely no basis whatsoever."

As with all other areas of international law, absence of political will and resolve among member states, combined with a lack of effective and centralized enforcement, has resulted in the process moving either painfully slowly, or not at all. Furthermore,

there is no international police force to impose the will of the international community in apprehending the accused. Hence, while some legal scholars have heralded the ad hoc tribunals as opening a new chapter in international law, others have claimed that their shortfalls have delivered a fatal blow to international justice.

As a relatively new development in international law, an increasing number of international rules are applied to individuals—in the domains of both human rights and war crimes. As a result, individuals can directly petition international bodies and bypass their national courts.

MILORAD KRNOJELAC

On June 25, 2001, Milorad Krnojelac, commander of the Foca Kazneno-Popravni Dom (KP Dom) from April 1992 to August 1993, was charged with 12 counts of crimes against humanity and violations of the laws or customs of war. Krnojelac was charged with acting together and in common purpose with the KP Dom guards to persecute Muslim and other non-Serb civilian detainees on political, racial, or religious grounds, commit acts of torture, beatings, and murder, and illegally detain non-Serb civilians.

The trial began October 30, 2000. Krnojelac was found responsible as an aider and abettor for the crime of persecution as a crime against humanity and the crime of cruel treatment as a violation of the laws or customs of war. Krnojelac was also held responsible for the crimes of persecution against humanity, inhumane acts as a crime against humanity, and cruel treatment as a violation of the laws or customs of war. He was acquitted on the counts of torture, murder, imprisonment, and other inhumane acts and given a single sentence of 7.5 years imprisonment.

Krnojelac appealed on April 12, 2002. He maintained his position as prison warden had been misevaluated. The appeals chamber found Krnojelac guilty as a co-perpetrator of persecution, a crime against humanity, and of cruel treatment, a violation of the laws or customs of war. It also found Krnojelac guilty of torture as a crime against humanity and a violation of the laws or customs of war and guilty of murder as a crime against humanity and as a violation of the laws or customs of war. The chamber revised Krnojelac's conviction to take into account newly discovered beatings. The chamber dismissed the sentencing appeals and imposed a new sentence of 15-years imprisonment.

At age 58, math teacher Milorad Krnojelac was made prison chief of KP Dom in Foca. Under his supervision the prisoners of KP Dom were beaten, starved, and terrorized.

KEY CONCEPTS

Nuremberg Trials From 1945 to 1946, an international military tribunal indicted and tried 22 former Nazi leaders as war criminals based on their crimes against humanity. The tribunal found overwhelming evidence of a systematic rule of violence, brutality, and terrorism by the German government in the territories occupied by its forces. The tribunal also found that atrocities had been committed on a large scale and as a matter of policy. Of the 24 individuals charged, 12 were sentenced to death by hanging, seven received prison terms ranging from 10 years to life, and three were acquitted.

The International Criminal Court

An effective international justice system requires that every state play its part in ensuring perpetrators of international crimes are brought to justice, regardless of whether that state has any connection to the crime concerned. Such universal jurisdiction means that state officials cannot claim **immunity** from prosecution if they are accused of international crimes.

Whether states have an obligation to bring such persons to trial has been another question. This debate was put to the test when Chile's former dictator, Augusto Pinochet, was detained in Great Britain in the late 1990s. The governments of Spain, Belgium, France, and Switzerland sought to try him for crimes of torture committed in Chile. The British government refused to extradite Pinochet,

or hand him over, on the grounds of ill health. Many commentators felt that if an international criminal court had existed at the time of the alleged crimes the legal arguments for extradition would have prevailed.

Since then, a permanent court has come into existence. The International Criminal Court (ICC) was agreed in principle at an international conference in Rome in July 1998.

■■■■ In June 2003, Luis Moreno-Ocampo took office as chief prosecutor of the International Criminal Court.

The noble aim of the new institution was to "end the gross violations of international humanitarian law that the past century has witnessed" and to ensure that such crimes were "no longer committed with impunity." Seven countries—China, Iraq, Israel, Libya, Qatar, the United States, and Yemen—voted against the statute, while 120 countries approved it. The treaty entered into force in July 2002, and 100 states were parties to the statute in 2005.

While the ICC is entirely independent of the UN, the UN Security Council can refer cases to it. It is also a court of last resort, meaning that, if there is a functioning legal system, all legal means in national courts must be first exhausted. Even then,

the ICC can only hear cases of crimes committed on the territory, or by a citizen of, the states that are parties to the treaty. Hence, although supported by a majority of countries, the ICC does not have universal jurisdiction. Supporters of such jurisdiction would argue that a war crime is a war crime and ought to be prosecuted wherever it occurs.

Although supported by a majority of countries, the ICC does not have universal jurisdiction.

While the United States helped draft much of the ICC treaty in order to address their national concerns, the United States is not a party to the treaty. Former U.S. president Bill Clinton signed the treaty in the closing days of his presidency, but the incoming administration of George W. Bush stated clearly that the United States did not intend to become a party to the treaty. Thus, the "U.S. has no legal obligations arising from its signature."

Defense Secretary Donald Rumsfeld explained that the administration had "a number of serious objections to the International Criminal Court, among them, the lack of adequate checks and balances on powers of the [Court's]

prosecutor and judges; the dilution of the UN Security Council's authority over international criminal prosecutions; and the lack of any effective mechanism to prevent politicized prosecutions of American service members and officials."

Supporters of the ICC say that many of these concerns have been addressed, largely due to the involvement of U.S. negotiators. Many safeguards are built into the court's proceedings to ensure that its jurisdiction is not overreached and that indictments are fair. If there were politically motivated charges, say supporters, the future of the court would be in jeopardy because states would not want to be subject to proceedings with a questionable legal basis. While some argue that the court will not be effective without the participation of the world's only superpower, the fact remains that the court is going ahead and that the United States—a primary defender of human rights—will have no say in its development.

Some opponents of the ICC claim that the court could try U.S. citizens without U.S. consent. Supporters say that this is a hollow legal claim because citizens are already prosecuted in foreign countries for crimes committed on foreign territory and foreign courts often have far fewer safeguards for protection of foreign nationals than would the ICC.

The Human Rights Revolution

Human rights laws and the incorporation of human rights principles into foreign policy are relatively new and revolutionary global developments. Before the 19th century, the principle that the rights of the individual should take precedence over national interests had rarely been proposed and had never been enacted. At one time, individuals were only under the jurisdiction of the states where they resided. States alone determined if an individual warranted diplomatic or judicial protection when abroad.

The first major departure from this practice came when Great Britain initiated the end of the slave trade in the early 1800s. Apart from some economic self-interest, it was recognized that an emerging international law should also protect individuals. Other human rights treaties followed, such as those adopted after World War I to protect workers' rights under the International Labor Organization (ILO).

Created after World War I in 1919, the ILO "seeks the promotion of social justice and internationally recognized human and labor rights." The ILO formulates international

---

International law remains based on western concepts of individual rights.

---

labor standards, setting minimum standards of basic labor rights. These rights include freedom of association, the right to organize, collective bargaining, abolition of forced labor, equality of opportunity and treatment, and other standards regulating conditions across the entire spectrum of work-related issues.

Yet, it was not until after World War II that the concept of international protection for individuals really took hold, due, in part, to the Holocaust. Since 1945, human rights law has been a growth industry. There have been more than 50 declarations and conventions of international and regional application to human rights. The central document is the Universal Declaration of Human Rights (UDHR), adopted in 1948. This declaration is fundamentally based on western political ideas and is in the form of

■■■ **Refugee camps must accommodate residents' sanitary, health, and nutritional needs.**

recommendations rather than requirements. As the first statement of its kind to confirm human dignity and to outline basic rights and freedoms, it was a landmark document. Prohibitions against slavery, torture, and arbitrary arrest, plus rights to expression, work, and education were among the many rights addressed in the declaration.

Near universal ratification of the UDHR is not to imply, however, that UN member states have unified views about the value of these rights. International law remains primarily Western in its orientation, based on Western concepts of individual rights. For countries such as China and Saudi Arabia, the secure functioning of society as a whole has a higher value than the promotion of the rights of any one individual. Disagreements over the status of such rights have been at the center of many UN debates.

Furthermore, Western states have emphasized civil and political rights, while the developing world has given primacy to economic and social rights. The UDHR principles on these rights were turned into more specific legal instruments in the form of the Covenant on Civil and Political Rights and the International Covenant on Economic, Social, and Cultural Rights, both adopted in 1966. As with all treaties, some of the biggest states have signed but not yet ratified these documents.

In the past, many states were wary of binding international adjudication, or legally binding settlement of international disputes by an impartial third party, in the area of human rights. Instead, the international community has encouraged voluntary compliance and has established an extensive monitoring process. The UN's Commission on Human Rights is charged with monitoring and reporting on human rights situations in various countries.

The UN will appoint special rapporteurs, or reporters, to investigate whether countries are living up to international standards on everything from violence against women to religious intolerance. Despite the legal limitations, the effect of drawing attention to gross violations of human rights should not be underestimated. When an offending state faces public pressure, policies can change.

Problems can arise, however, when a state commits an act such as genocide and claims that this is a matter for its own domestic jurisdiction. As with many other debates about international law, the tension between national sovereignty and universal standards remains. Article 55 in the UN charter

███ **The United Nations Operation in Somalia was a year-long mission providing humanitarian assistance to civilians following the cease-fire in Mogadishu.**

FROM THE UNIVERSAL DECLARATION OF HUMAN RIGHTS

Article 1
All human beings are born free and equal in dignity and rights. They are endowed with reason and conscience and should act towards one another in a spirit of brotherhood.

Article 3
Everyone has the right to life, liberty, and security of person.

Article 4
No one shall be held in slavery or servitude; slavery and the slave trade shall be prohibited in all their forms.

Article 5
No one shall be subjected to torture or to cruel, inhuman or degrading treatment or punishment.

Article 9
No one shall be subjected to arbitrary arrest, detention or exile.

Article 13
(1) Everyone has the right to freedom of movement and residence within the borders of each state.
(2) Everyone has the right to leave any country, including his own, and to return to his country.

Article 18
Everyone has the right to freedom of thought, conscience and religion; this right includes freedom to change his religion or belief, and freedom, either alone or in community with others and in public or private, to manifest his religion or belief in teaching, practice, worship and observance.

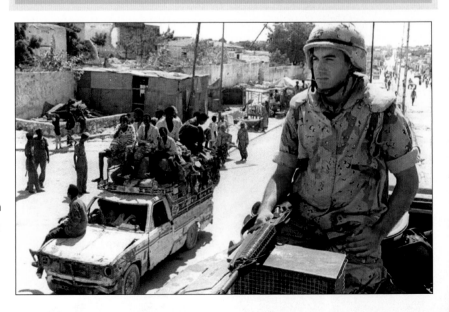

specifies that the UN shall promote "universal respect for, and observance of, human rights and fundamental freedoms for all without distinction as to race, sex, language or religion." On the other hand, Article 2 (7) notes that "nothing contained in the present Charter shall authorize the UN to intervene in matters which are essentially within the domestic jurisdiction of any state." Regardless of this seeming contradiction, when the member states of the UN determine that human rights violations are on a scale to cause a "threat to international peace and security," enforcement actions can be taken according to Chapter VII guidelines.

The trend to intervene for humanitarian purposes is an entirely new development in international law and one that the international community still wrestles with, especially when faced with operations like Restore Hope in Somalia in 1992. This UN-authorized, but U.S.-led mission was meant to provide security for the delivery of humanitarian supplies. However, its objectives were not achieved — the UN troops were

---

Operation Restore Hope in Somalia in 1992 was largely judged a debacle.

---

defeated by warlords and were withdrawn without having reestablished order. While there has been increasing acceptance of the doctrine that massive human rights abuses warrant external intervention, there is far less consensus on who should intervene, on what terms, and to accomplish which ends.

Of course, before a last resort of forcible intervention is attempted, there are other options available to the international community, such as trade or diplomatic sanctions. One of the most notable examples is the range of economic and political sanctions placed on South Africa (1977–1994) for its human rights violations under an apartheid regime. The argument against sanctions, however, is that they can significantly harm the civilian populations they are designed to help. Critics note that the economic embargo imposed on Iraq after the Gulf War ended in 1991 did little to affect the political establishment. The embargo has instead devastated the economy and caused great suffering for the Iraqi people. The debate about the utility of sanctions is ongoing.

KEY CONCEPTS

Sanctions The UN charter describes sanctions as complete or partial interruption of economic relations and of air, postal, rail, radio, sea, telegraphic, and other means of communication, and the severance of diplomatic relations. Sanctions can severely damage a country's economy. Today, there is much controversy surrounding the use of sanctions. While some consider sanctions to be a means of solving conflict without the use of military force, others claim that

sanctions are more damaging to a country's citizens than to the leaders they are supposed to punish. Between 1991 and 1996, for example, economic sanctions placed upon Iraq are estimated to have resulted in the deaths of more than 500,000 children from starvation and a lack of medical care.

The UN and Human Rights
Virtually every part of the UN is involved in protecting human rights to some degree. One of

the UN's greatest achievements is the creation of a comprehensive body of human rights law that provides a universal and internationally protected code of human rights to which all nations can subscribe and all people can aspire. Human rights are considered fundamental to modern society. They are the basic rights of an individual and include the right to be born, the right to live, and the right to work, among others.

Mapping Treaties

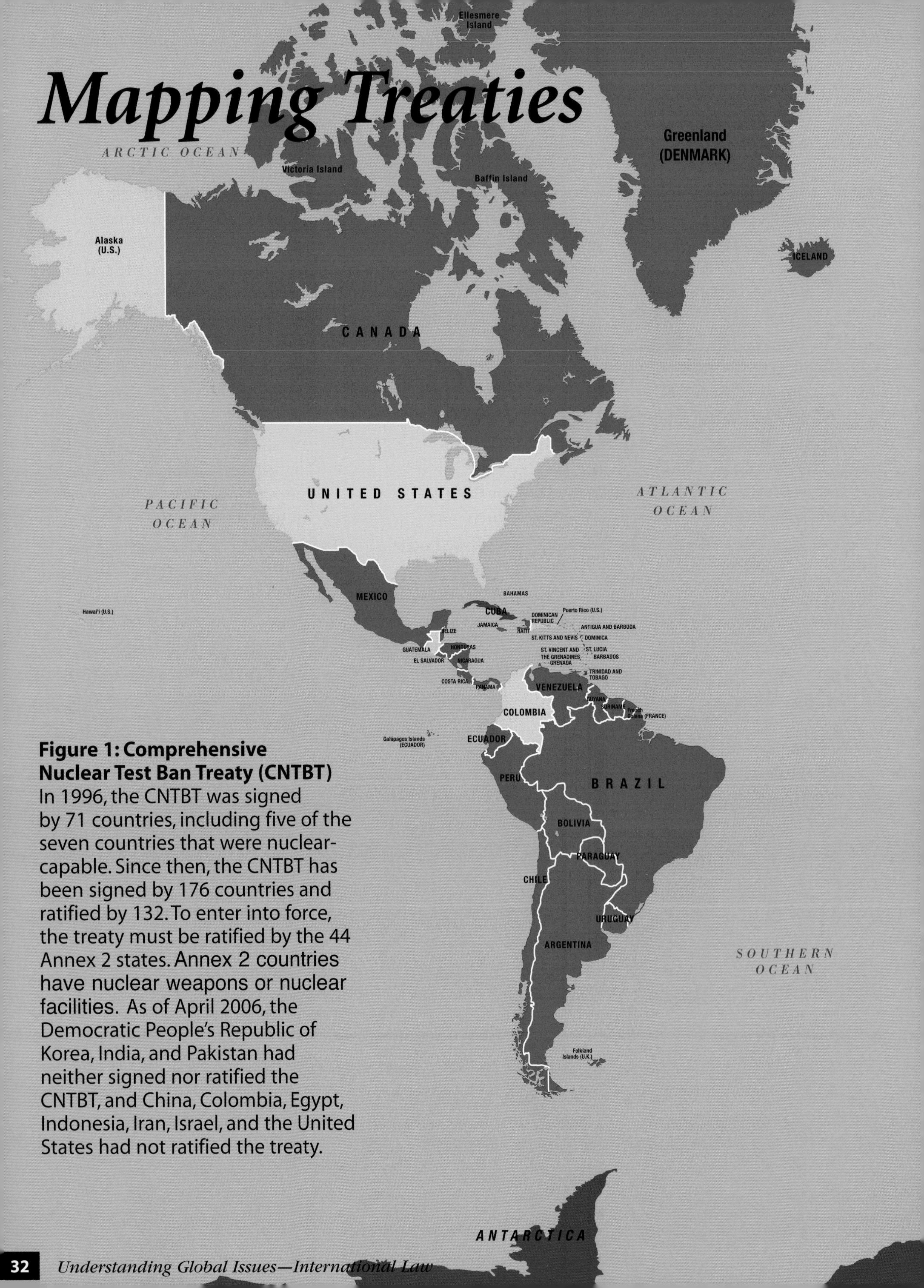

ARCTIC OCEAN

Ellesmere Island

Greenland (DENMARK)

Victoria Island

Baffin Island

ICELAND

Alaska (U.S.)

C A N A D A

PACIFIC OCEAN

UNITED STATES

ATLANTIC OCEAN

Hawai'i (U.S.)

MEXICO

BAHAMAS

CUBA

DOMINICAN REPUBLIC

Puerto Rico (U.S.)

ANTIGUA AND BARBUDA

JAMAICA

HAITI

ST. KITTS AND NEVIS   DOMINICA

BELIZE

GUATEMALA

HONDURAS

ST. VINCENT AND   ST. LUCIA

THE GRENADINES   BARBADOS

GRENADA

EL SALVADOR

NICARAGUA

COSTA RICA

TRINIDAD AND TOBAGO

PANAMA

VENEZUELA

GUYANA

SURINAME

COLOMBIA

French Guiana (FRANCE)

Galápagos Islands (ECUADOR)

ECUADOR

PERU

B R A Z I L

BOLIVIA

PARAGUAY

CHILE

URUGUAY

ARGENTINA

SOUTHERN OCEAN

Falkland Islands (U.K.)

ANTARCTICA

Figure 1: Comprehensive Nuclear Test Ban Treaty (CNTBT)

In 1996, the CNTBT was signed by 71 countries, including five of the seven countries that were nuclear-capable. Since then, the CNTBT has been signed by 176 countries and ratified by 132. To enter into force, the treaty must be ratified by the 44 Annex 2 states. Annex 2 countries have nuclear weapons or nuclear facilities. As of April 2006, the Democratic People's Republic of Korea, India, and Pakistan had neither signed nor ratified the CNTBT, and China, Colombia, Egypt, Indonesia, Iran, Israel, and the United States had not ratified the treaty.

ARCTIC OCEAN

Spitsbergen (NORWAY)

Novaja Zemlya

Ostrov Anzu

RUSSIA

FINLAND

NORWAY   SWEDEN

ESTONIA
LATVIA
LITHUANIA
DENMARK
IRELAND
UNITED KINGDOM
NETHERLANDS
BELGIUM
LUXEMBOURG
GERMANY
POLAND   BELARUS

RUSSIA

KAZAKHSTAN

MONGOLIA

NORTH KOREA

JAPAN

FRANCE   CZECH REPUBLIC
AUSTRIA
SWITZERLAND   SLOVENIA
HUNGARY
SLOVAKIA
ROMANIA
MOLDOVA
UKRAINE

UZBEKISTAN
KYRGYZSTAN
TURKMENISTAN   TAJIKISTAN

CHINA

SOUTH KOREA

PACIFIC OCEAN

PORTUGAL   SPAIN
ANDORRA
ITALY
CROATIA
BOSNIA AND HERZEGOVINA
SERBIA AND MONTENEGRO
ALBANIA
GREECE
MALTA

BULGARIA
MACEDONIA
GEORGIA
ARMENIA
AZERBAIJAN
TURKEY

CYPRUS
SYRIA
LEBANON
ISRAEL/OTAT
JORDAN

IRAN

AFGHANISTAN

NEPAL
BHUTAN

Taiwan

Gibraltar (U.K.)

TUNISIA

MOROCCO

ALGERIA

LIBYA

EGYPT

IRAQ
KUWAIT
BAHRAIN
SAUDI ARABIA
QATAR
UNITED ARAB EMIRATES
OMAN

YEMEN

PAKISTAN

INDIA

BANGLADESH

MYANMAR (BURMA)

LAOS

THAILAND   VIETNAM

Western Sahara

MAURITANIA

MALI   NIGER

CHAD

SUDAN

ERITREA
DJIBOUTI

ETHIOPIA

SOMALIA

SRI LANKA

CAMBODIA

PHILIPPINES

PALAU

SENEGAL
GAMBIA
GUINEA-BISSAU   GUINEA
SIERRA LEONE
LIBERIA

BURKINA FASO
BENIN
TOGO
IVORY COAST (CÔTE D'IVOIRE)
GHANA

NIGERIA

CAMEROON

CENTRAL AFRICAN REPUBLIC

UGANDA   KENYA

BRUNEI

MALAYSIA

EQUATORIAL GUINEA
SAO TOME AND PRINCIPE
GABON
REPUBLIC OF THE CONGO

CABINDA

DEMOCRATIC REPUBLIC OF THE CONGO

RWANDA
BURUNDI

TANZANIA

INDONESIA

East Timor (Timor-Leste)

PAPUA NEW GUINEA

ANGOLA   ZAMBIA

MALAWI

COMOROS

ZIMBABWE

MOZAMBIQUE

MADAGASCAR

INDIAN OCEAN

NAMIBIA   BOTSWANA

SWAZILAND

LESOTHO

SOUTH AFRICA

AUSTRALIA

N

SCALE AT EQUATOR

| 0 | 1,000 | 2,000 | 3,000 miles |
| 0 | 1,609 | 3,219 | 4,828 kilometers |

LEGEND

☐ Signed

◼ Signed and Ratified

◼ Not Signed and Not Ratified

Source: The Preparatory Commission for the Comprehensive Nuclear-Test-Ban Treaty Organization (CTBTO Preparatory Commission)

Charting International Law

Figure 2: Kyoto Protocol

The Kyoto Protocol to the Framework Convention on Climate Change was agreed upon in December 1997, opened for signature on March 16, 1998, and closed on March 15, 1999. The agreement came into force on February 16, 2005, following ratification by Russia on November 18, 2004.

As of April 2006, a total of 163 countries have ratified the agreement (representing more than 61.6 percent of emissions from Annex I countries, which are divided into six geographical regions to ensure geographical balance). Notable exceptions include the United States and Australia. Other countries, such as India and China, which have ratified the protocol, are not required to reduce carbon emissions under the present agreement.

- ◼ Signature
- ◼ Signature and Annex 1 Party
- ◻ No Signature
- ◼ No Information Available

Source: United Nations Framework Convention on Climate Change

Figure 3:
Human Rights Treaties
A number of human rights treaties have been proposed over the years. While many states have been parties to the treaties, not all have ratified them. The chart on the right shows the number of countries that have ratified six major human rights treaties.

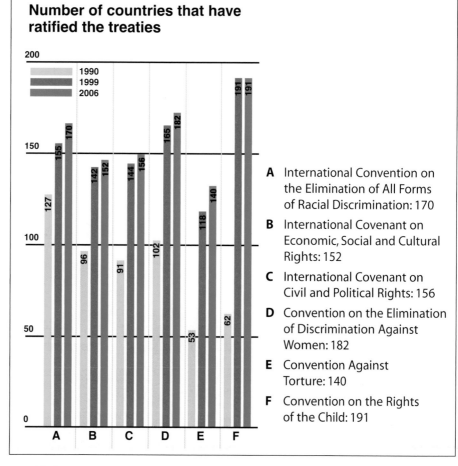

Number of countries that have ratified the treaties

Legend:
- 1990
- 1999
- 2006

Values (1990 / 1999 / 2006):
- A: 127 / 155 / 170
- B: 96 / 142 / 152
- C: 91 / 144 / 156
- D: 102 / 165 / 182
- E: 53 / 118 / 140
- F: 62 / 191 / 191

A International Convention on the Elimination of All Forms of Racial Discrimination: 170

B International Covenant on Economic, Social and Cultural Rights: 152

C International Covenant on Civil and Political Rights: 156

D Convention on the Elimination of Discrimination Against Women: 182

E Convention Against Torture: 140

F Convention on the Rights of the Child: 191

Figure 4: The UN and Human Rights
Various mechanisms exist at the UN to protect individuals from the violations of human rights committed by erring or oppressive governments. The process can, however, be both daunting and subject to political manipulation.

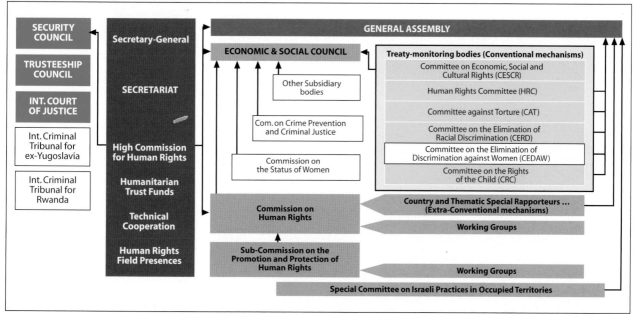

Law and the Environment

Environmental law came into its own in the 1960s, when public opinion began to crystallize around the idea that industrial and military pollution by states was causing large-scale damage to the environment, and that this pollution had no respect for borders. There is now a much greater awareness of the repercussions of slash-and-burn agriculture, the dumping of toxic wastes, and soil erosion. The environmental movement received new ammunition with events such as the incident that occurred at a Chernobyl nuclear plant in the former Soviet Union in 1986 and the grounding of the Exxon Valdez oil tanker in 1988, which polluted more than 1,000 miles (1,609 kilometers) of Alaska's coastline. After events such as these, it was increasingly difficult for states to argue that they had no responsibility for the global environment because pollution crosses borders.

Despite this change of thinking about international law regarding the environment, state interests remain paramount. In other words, a state generally will want to exploit natural resources for its own benefit and limit social and economic costs as

■■■ In 1986, the explosion that rocked Chernobyl, then part of the USSR, was the worst nuclear incident the world had seen.

much as possible. Largely for financial reasons, states are reluctant to admit responsibility for environmental damage. They argue that it is often very difficult to determine fair compensation when extensive harm to the environment is concerned.

The scientific data on the environmental impacts of human activities are also conflicting. For all of these reasons, states take a very cautious approach when it comes to environmental agreements. Many conventions

---

States take a very cautious approach when it comes to environmental agreements.

---

and protocols that have set environmental standards have yet to enter into force because of inadequate ratification.

Implementing the standards set in these treaties at the national level is another hardship. New national legislation may be required to ensure international standards can be applied within a national legal system. Domestic politics weigh heavily on such decisions. If the proposed agreement means any increase in oil, gas, or electricity prices, states are not likely to welcome the change. In most of these agreements, then, each country

tends to define compliance in whatever way best serves its national interest.

As with human rights law, developed and developing nations also have very different perspectives when it comes to environmental rules. Developing countries claim that developed countries are the biggest polluters. The United States, with 4.5 percent of the world's population, produces approximately 25 percent of **greenhouse gases**. Developing countries question the fairness of having tough environmental requirements imposed upon them that would potentially restrict their economic growth. For their part, developed countries have little inclination to lower their standard of living to conform to more equitable global rules.

Due to the fact that many states are especially averse to binding agreements where the global environment is concerned, many such treaties take the form of framework agreements, which means that they only provide a framework for further negotiations, such as the Framework Convention on Climate Change, which entered into force in 1994. The convention required that states report on emissions of green-house gases.

There was very little that states could agree on with respect to this subject due, in part, to very different economic situations. As such, the convention set up a framework for agreeing to specific actions.

Several other international instruments have been designed to obtain a consensus on environmental issues, but they are not regarded as legally binding. These include the 1972 Stockholm Declaration, the 1982 World Charter for Nature, and the 1992 Rio Declaration on the Environment and Development. These resolutions and declarations are also known as soft law. One Internet site lists more than 650 of these agreements on the topic of the environment alone. When it comes to environmental law, the emphasis is much less on binding jurisdiction and much more on ensuring that mechanisms are set up to monitor states' compliance with international standards.

The UN Environment Program (UNEP) is the main body that oversees international agreements and promotes compliance with existing laws. Monitoring the illegal trade in wild flora and fauna is one example of the institution's tasks. Such work requires close collaboration with Interpol, the World Customs Organization, and the enforcement agencies

---

The convention set up a framework for agreeing to specific actions.

---

of different countries. While this watchdog role is important, UNEP has little power to impose or enforce sanctions on noncomplying states. More than 80 governments approved the Guidelines on Compliance with and Enforcement of Multilateral Environmental Agreements, adopted by UNEPs

Governing Council in February 2002. It was also made quite clear that these guidelines were advisory and not binding. In fact, the text notes that "states are best placed to choose the approaches that are useful and appropriate for enhancing compliance with multilateral environmental agreements."

This statement alone shows the obvious problems with the enforcement of any global environmental standards.

Despite the enforcement problem and reluctant half measures for some treaties such as the Kyoto Protocol, there are occasional success stories. Agreements to protect the stratospheric ozone layer under the Montreal Protocol on Substances that Deplete the Ozone Layer resulted in a drastic reduction in the production of chlorofluorocarbons, which are known to damage the ozone layer. This agreement was considered a landmark international negotiation.

KEY CONCEPTS

Soft Law Agreements on principles with little official legal force are referred to as soft law. Often, these agreements are laid out in declarations, and charters, reflecting ethical conceptions that have not yet found their way into law. Soft law is becoming important because judges are starting to use soft law principles as a basis for their rulings. The development of soft law has been strongly stimulated by a number of global conferences and summits, such as the Conference on Environment and Development in Rio de Janeiro, the Social Summit in Copenhagen, and the Conference on Demography in Cairo.

Montreal Protocol on Substances that Deplete the Ozone Layer Following the discovery of the Antarctic ozone hole in late 1985, governments recognized the need for stronger measures to reduce the production and consumption of a number of chlorofluorocarbons, which are gases used as refrigerants and in aerosols. The protocol was adopted on September 16, 1987, and came into force on January 1, 1989, when it was ratified by 29 countries and the European Economic Community (EEC). Since then, several other countries have ratified the protocol.

International Lawyer

Duties: Counsel clients about legal rights and obligations, suggest courses of action in business matters, represent clients in court proceedings

Education: Bachelor of Laws or Juris Doctor degree; Master of Laws (LL.M.) degree, either specifically in international law or with focus upon international law

Interests: International relations, debate, research, and analysis

Visit the American Society of International Law at **www.asil. org/** to learn more about careers in international law. Also click on **www.uianet.org/index.jsp** to visit the International Association of Lawyers website.

Careers in Focus

Lawyers act as advisors and advocates in society. As advisors, they counsel their clients about legal rights and obligations. As advocates, they represent parties in court, presenting evidence and arguing a case. In both capacities, lawyers must be knowledgeable about the intent of laws and past judicial decisions. They must also be able to apply the law to specific circumstances their clients face.

Obtaining a law degree is the first step to becoming an international lawyer. Lawyers must also pass a special examination, called the bar examination, to be eligible to practice law. A master's degree in international affairs or a related field supplements the knowledge of a prospective international lawyer. Foreign languages, such as French, German, Japanese, Russian, and Spanish, can be beneficial. International lawyers must also be familiar with the cultures of different areas of the world.

Essential skills for international lawyers include analytical ability, research and writing skills, and knowledge of the basic differences in the world's legal systems and their political and cultural contexts.

International lawyers can work for law firms, federal governments, international organizations, and nonprofit groups. Private law firms handle international business transactions. Law firms with foreign offices often send international lawyers to serve in these offices.

The European Union: A Model for the Future?

The European Union (EU) represents the largest pool of national sovereignty in world history. It is becoming a testing ground for the development of international law. Before World War II, international law primarily defined trade relations between states and the limits of aggression in times of war. Since then, it has broadened its reach to include laws covering the environment and, in particular,

human rights. International law is no longer limited to relations between states; individuals, too, can come within its scope.

> *Individuals, too, can come within the scope of international law.*

The role of nongovernmental organizations (NGOs) is also growing. The Landmines

Convention became international law in early 1999 through NGO pressure, not because of UN action.

Nevertheless, international law without a means to enforce it is deeply flawed. Nation states vary in their willingness to be bound by it—witness the ongoing difficulties with controlling the proliferation of nuclear weapons and other weapons of mass destruction. The underlying issue is

■■■ **In December 2000, the Charter of Fundamental Rights of the European Union was adopted, making each member state subject to the same human rights standards.**

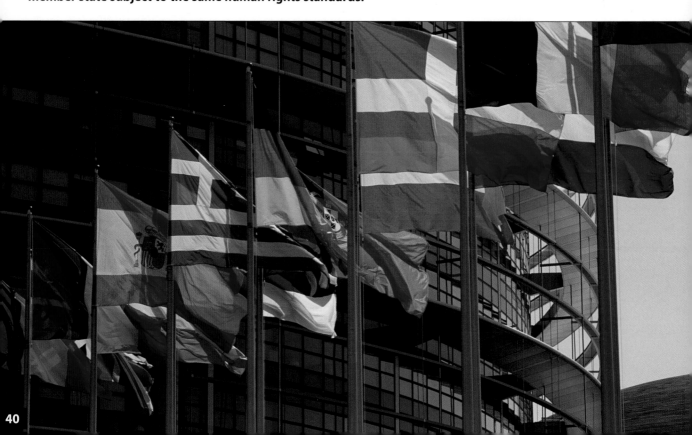

sovereignty and how much countries are willing to relinquish for the greater good. This, in turn, depends in large part on a recognition by nations that the values they have in common are more important than those which divide them. In this regard, Europe offers a unique case study.

Since 1951, the European Union and its forerunners have created a very substantial body of laws, known as the *acquis communautaire*, which supersedes the national laws of member countries, but are enforced in these countries' national courts. The European Court of Justice, the ultimate court of appeal, has the duty of ensuring that these laws are applied uniformly in all member states.

In the realm of human rights law, the judicial system in Europe is unique in that, unlike other bodies at the international level, the decisions of the European Court of Human Rights, created by the Council of Europe, are final and binding on the states that have signed the 1950 European Convention on Human Rights. In 2006, all 46 member states of the Council of Europe had signed this convention. In some states, the provisions

---

The European Court of Justice has the duty of ensuring laws are applied uniformly in all member states.

---

of the convention are part of domestic law. In others, the state must ensure that domestic law conforms to its responsibilities under the convention. States found in breach of their obligations are required to make the necessary changes in their legal systems.

EU social law is also unique. The Amsterdam Treaty, which entered into force in May 1999, built on the social elements of the Maastricht Treaty, which in turn embodied much of the groundwork developed by the Council of Europe. The Amsterdam Treaty identified the promotion of improved living and working conditions as an EU objective and transferred asylum, immigration, and civil judicial policy to the EU's jurisdiction. For such matters to be centralized at a supranational level is unprecedented.

The path towards EU integration has not been smooth. On October 29, 2004, EU member state heads of government and state signed the treaty establishing a constitution for Europe. This has been ratified by 13 member states and is currently awaiting ratification by the other states. However, this process faltered on May 29, 2005, when the majority of French voters rejected the constitution in a referendum by 54.7 percent. The French rejection was followed by a Dutch rejection three days later when 61.6 percent of Dutch voters refused the constitution as well. The current and future status of the European Union therefore continues to be subject of political controversy, with widely differing views both within and between member states.

The U.S.-led war in Iraq in 2003 exposed real divisions between EU governments over foreign policy and the interpretation of international law. The EU's real success in developing strong institutions and enforceable laws has been tarnished, however, in the eyes of outside observers by the actions of member nations over some high-profile external issues: protectionist—and allegedly illegal—measures against agricultural imports, foreign ownership of the media, and bending the rules on budgetary deficits.

Twenty-five countries belong to the European Union and are part of the European Parliament, which has more than 700 representatives.

At the December 2005 Intergovernmental Conference (IGC), a semi-annual meeting, EU member states decided how it should allocate the EU budget for the next seven years (2007-2013). The "Financial Perspective" was defined as EU members agreed to fix the common budget to 1.045 percent of the European gross domestic product (GDP). British Prime Minister Tony Blair agreed to review the British rebate, negotiated by Margaret Thatcher in 1984, despite a promise made to the contrary. French President Jacques Chirac declared that this increase in budget would permit Europe to "finance common policies" such as the Common Agricultural Policy or the Research and Technological Development Policy. However, France's demand to lower the value added tax (VAT) in catering was refused.

EUROPEAN UNION LANGUAGES

The languages of the European Union are used by people within the member states. They include the 20 official languages of the European Union and many others. The EU asserts on its English language homepage, "languages: such as Europe's asset."

EU policy is to encourage all its citizens to be multilingual. Specifically, it encourages them to be able to speak two languages in addition to their mother tongue. A number of EU funding programs actively promote language learning and linguistic diversity, but the EU has very limited influence in this area as the content of educational systems remains the responsibility of individual member states.

According to the EU's English language website, the cost of maintaining its policy of multilingualism is 1.05 percent of the annual general budget of the EU, or 2.28 Euros per person per year.

THE COUNCIL OF EUROPE

The treaty setting up the Council of Europe was signed in London in 1949. Following the horrors of World War II, its purpose was to "achieve a greater unity between its Members for the purpose of safeguarding and realizing the ideals and principles which are their common heritage, and facilitating their economic and social progress."

The treaty was signed by 10 countries: Belgium, Denmark, France, Ireland, Italy, Luxembourg, the Netherlands, Norway, Sweden, and Great Britain. West Germany joined two years later. The Council's first major acts were the European Convention on Human Rights (ECHR) and the creation of the European Court of Human Rights to enforce its provisions.

The treaty made no mention of political, economic, or defense integration, and in 1951, Belgium, France, Germany, Italy, Luxembourg, and the Netherlands signed the Treaty of Rome. This treaty created the Coal and Steel Community, which intended to promote an ever-closer political and economic union between its members.

Any European nation can join the Council of Europe provided "it accepts the principle of the rule of law and guarantees human rights and fundamental freedoms to everyone under its jurisdiction." After 1986, most of the Eastern European nations joined, the latest being Serbia and Montenegro in April 2003. As of April 2006, the council had 46 members.

Since 1949, the council has evolved into a large body of conventions and protocols covering social and cultural issues. Apart from the ECHR, these are not backed by any judicial force, but the council remains the major forum for debating and expressing the shared cultural values at the heart of most EU law.

On the wider world stage, the policy-forming role of the council is played by UNESCO and other UN institutions, but common ground is clearly much harder to achieve among 191 UN member nations whose cultural, political, and religious values are so varied and often fundamentally incompatible.

All EU member states are also members of the Council of Europe. The Council of Europe defends human rights, monitors environmental issues, and encourages cultural understanding.

The International Committee of the Red Cross has been awarded the Nobel Peace Prize three times.

KEY CONCEPTS

The European Convention on Human Rights This convention is based on the Universal Declaration of Human Rights. Contracting states undertake to ensure a number of civil and political rights and freedoms set out in the convention to everyone within their jurisdiction. Subsequent protocols have extended the initial list of rights,

and the case law of the European Court and European Commission of Human Rights have reinforced and developed these rights.

Nongovernmental Organizations (NGOs)
Nongovernmental organizations (NGOs) do not belong to any political party and are not affiliated with any government

body. These nonprofit organizations are typically run by volunteers. NGOs often represent special interests, such as the environment or human rights. Increasingly, the UN is cooperating with NGOs in its efforts to create a civil society for all. More than 1,500 NGOs cooperate with the UN and share information.

Duties: Translate and interpret written text and live speech from one language to another
Education: Bachelor of Arts in main language, skilled knowledge of three of the six official UN languages
Interests: Languages, working with people, and cultures

Navigate to **www.calmis.cahw net.gov/file/occguide/ Translat.htm** for more information about careers in translation and interpretation. Also visit **http://portal.unesco.org/en** and click on Employment, then Translators & Interpreters.

Careers in Focus

Translators and interpreters are interested in the translation of spoken or written words and expressions from one language to another. There is a difference between the work of a translator and interpreter. Translators deal with written text. This means that they write documents in another language. Interpreters work with live speech. They listen as people speak and interpret what they say. Translators and interpreters must be extremely fluent in the languages they translate, and they must have an excellent understanding of the subject matter.

The work of the translator falls into three categories: literary, legal, and scientific and technical. A UN translator works mainly in the legal area, translating laws, foreign court orders, and treaties. The work of the translator is very important because they must translate ambiguous and unclear statements.

Interpreters can work in two different ways. The interpreter may interpret consecutively, which means he or she wait for the speaker to pause to interpret what has been said. The interpreter may also work simultaneously, which means he or she translates continuously while the person is talking. Simultaneous interpreting is required of court and international conference interpreters. It is much more difficult than consecutive interpreting. When simultaneous interpreting occurs, the interpreter needs to be able to anticipate what the speaker will say next, as well as the ability to speak and listen at the same time.

Timeline of Events

1648

The treaty of the Peace of Westphalia formalizes the concept of territorial sovereignty of nation-states.

1815

The Congress of Vienna clarifies relationships between European powers.

1864

The first Geneva Convention is adopted. It provides for protection of sick and wounded soldiers on the battlefield.

1920

The Covenant for a League of Nations is drawn up in an attempt to institutionalize a set of rules for a community of nations beyond Europe.

1945–1946

The Nuremberg Trials take place. Twenty-two former Nazi leaders are tried as war criminals for their crimes against humanity.

1946

The International Court of Justice is inaugurated on April 18.

1948

The UN General Assembly adopts the Universal Declaration of Human Rights.

1948

The UN Genocide Convention is established, providing a legal definition of genocide and establishing it as a crime under international law. The convention takes effect in 1951.

1980

The Vienna Convention on the Law of Treaties is entered into force. The convention requires states to adhere to core international values over and above national claims.

1992

An ICJ ruling establishes new boundaries between Honduras and El Salvador.

1993

On May 25, the UN Security Council establishes the International Criminal Tribunal for the former Yugoslavia (ICTY). The ICTY establishes that war crimes committed in civil wars are now subject to prosecution.

1994

The UN Security Council creates the International Criminal Tribunal for Rwanda (ICTR) on November 8.

1995

The ICTR issues its first indictment against eight accused persons on November 28.

1997

The Kyoto Protocol to the Framework Convention on Climate Change is agreed upon. It is entered into force on February 16, 2005.

2001

Following the Afghanistan War, 660 unlawful enemy combatants from 42 countries are detained in Cuba by the United States. The detainees are not legally prisoners of war and, therefore, are not protected by the Geneva Conventions.

■■■ Guantanamo Bay, Cuba, a prison for international criminal suspects, has brought the United States under scrutiny as many claim some activities on the base violate aspects of the Geneva Convention.

2003

In March, the International Criminal Court is inaugurated.

2003

The United States suspends military aid to South Africa following a South African government decision to not grant Americans immunity from prosecution by the ICC.

2004

On February 23, the ICJ begins hearings on Israel's barrier in the West Bank. Israel is building the wall to block suicide bombers, but it is building it on Palestinian territory.

2005

Spain votes to ratify the European Constitution, but France and the Netherlands vote to reject it.

2006

The United States signs a civilian nuclear pact with India. The agreement provides an exemption for India from U.S. laws limiting trade with countries that have refused to sign the nuclear Non-Proliferation Treaty (NPT).

Concept Web

Nuremberg War
Crimes Tribunal

International Criminal
Tribunal for the former
Yugoslavia (ICTY)

International
Criminal Tribunal
for Rwanda (CICTR)

Enforcement

**Nongovernmental
Organizations
(NGOs)**

**International
Criminal Court
(ICC)**

INTERNATIONAL LAW

Independent of UN

Environment

League of Nations

UN Environment
Programme (UNEP)

Not supported by
several big powers

Human Rights

UN's commission
on Human Rights

International Labor
Organization (ILO)

Universal Declaration
of Human Rights

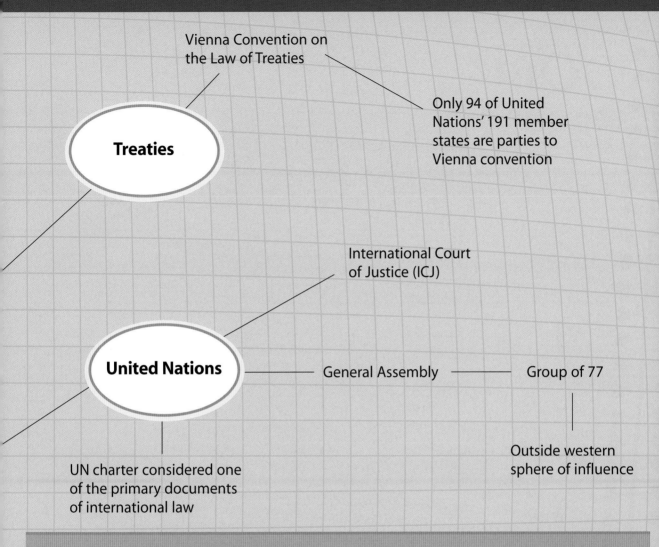

Treaties

Vienna Convention on the Law of Treaties

Only 94 of United Nations' 191 member states are parties to Vienna convention

United Nations

International Court of Justice (ICJ)

General Assembly ——— Group of 77

Outside western sphere of influence

UN charter considered one of the primary documents of international law

MAKE YOUR OWN CONCEPT WEB

A concept web is a useful summary tool. It can also be used to plan your research or help you write an essay or report. To make your own concept web, follow the steps below:

- You will need a large piece of unlined paper and a pencil.
- First, read through your source material, such as *International Law* in the Understanding Global Issues series.
- Write the main idea, or concept, in large letters in the center of the page.
- On a sheet of lined paper, jot down all words, phrases, or lists that you know are connected with the concept. Try to do this from memory.
- Look at your list. Can you group your words and phrases in certain topics or themes? Connect the different topics with lines to the center, or to other "branches."
- Critique your concept web. Ask questions about the material on your concept web: Does it all make sense? Are all the links shown? Could there be other ways of looking at it? Is anything missing?
- What more do you need to find out? Develop questions for those areas you are still unsure about or where information is missing. Use these questions as a basis for further research.

Quiz

Multiple Choice

1. Where did international law develop?
   a) among Muslims as Islamic law
   b) among the early nation-states of Europe
   c) in the United Nations, following World War I
   d) in North America

2. Which of the following countries have not accepted the authority of the International Court of Justice?
   a) the United States
   b) India
   c) Great Britain
   d) Egypt

3. The International Court of Justice was inaugurated on:
   a) January 1, 1980.
   b) March 31, 2003.
   c) April 18, 1946.
   d) May 25, 1993.

4. The Covenant for a League of Nations:
   a) was an attempt to institutionalize a set of rules for a community of nations beyond Europe
   b) ultimately failed because several big powers failed to support it
   c) established mechanisms for the arbitration of international disputes
   d) all of the above

5. The International Criminal Tribunal for the former Yugoslavia indicted this key figure:
   a) Pol Pot
   b) Ratko Mladic
   c) Slobodan Milosevic
   d) The tribunal has not issued any judgements to date.

6. The Group of 77, the largest Third World coalition in the United Nations, is made up of countries from:
    a) South America and Asia
    b) Africa, Asia, and Latin America
    c) Asia and Latin America
    d) Africa and Asia

7. According to international law, resorting to force for self-defense is permissible:
    a) when a state fears an armed attack and can provide proof that such an attack is imminent
    b) never
    c) self-defense does not have to be justified
    d) only to repel an armed attack

Where Did It Happen?

1. The Charter of the United Nations was signed here.
2. Operation Restore Hope in 1992 failed in this country.
3. The International Criminal Court was inaugurated here in March 2003.
4. This group of sovereign nations has created a body of laws that supersedes the national laws of member countries.

True or False

1. The United Nations supports the use of force for self-defense purposes.
2. UN member states must register treaties with the United Nations if they wish to bring a case before the International Court of Justice.
3. The International Criminal Tribunal for the former Yugoslavia and the International Criminal Tribunal for Rwanda have been praised for dispensing quick justice.
4. The International Criminal Court is a UN body.

Answers on page 53

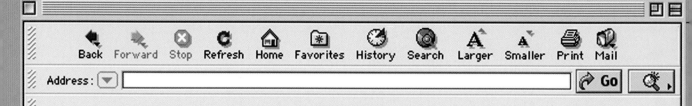

Internet Resources

The following websites provide more information about international law:

The United Nations International Law
www.un.org/law/index.html
The United Nations has a web page dedicated to international law. From this page, you can click on the many links to learn about the role of treaties in international law and how the two international courts—the ICJ and the ICC—function. You can also explore in detail the latest developments of the ICTY and ICTR.

Encarta
http://encarta.msn.com
Visit the Encarta online encyclopedia to learn more about international law. You can type terms such as "International Criminal Court," "European Union," or "Kyoto Protocol" into the search engine.

Some websites stay current longer than others. To find other international law websites, enter terms such as "International Court of Justice," "war crimes," or "treaties" into a search engine.

Further Reading

Gray, Christine. *International Law and the Use of Force.* New York: Oxford Press, 2001.

Maguire, Peter H. *Law and War.* New York: Columbia University Press, 2002.

McCormick, John. *The European Union: Politics and Policies.* New York: Westview Press, 1999.

Persico, Joseph E. *Nuremberg: Infamy on Trial.* New York: Penguin USA, 1995.

Schabas, William A. *An Introduction to the International Criminal Court.* New York: Cambridge University Press, 2004.

Answers

Multiple Choice
1. b) 2. a) 3. c) 4. d) 5. c) 6. b) 7. d)

Where Did It Happen?
1. San Francisco, United States. 2. Somalia 3. The Hague, Netherlands
4. The European Union

True or False
1. T 2. T 3. F 4. F

Glossary

ad hoc: done or set up solely in response to a particular situation or problem without considering wider issues

anarchy: a society without a formal system of government

case law: law established on the basis of previous verdicts

Cold War: the tensions that developed between the United States and the Union of Soviet Socialist Republics from the end of World War II through 1989

colonial: one country's political domination of another country or people—usually achieved through aggressive, often military, actions—and the territory acquired in this manner

developed countries: countries in the industrialized world; highly economically and technologically developed

ethnic cleansing: the expulsion, imprisonment, or killing of ethnic minorities by a dominant majority group

genocide: systematic measures for the extermination of a national, cultural, religious, or racial group

greenhouse gases: atmospheric gases that can reflect heat back to Earth

immunity: an exemption from prosecution for someone who has knowledge of possible criminal activity and may be personally culpable in exchange for giving sufficient information to the police or to a grand jury

indicted: formally charged with committing a crime

jurisdiction: the area over which legal authority extends

multilateral: involving two or more nations

nation-states: independent states recognized by, and capable of interacting with, other states, often composed of people of the same nationalities

Security Council: the branch of the United Nations that maintains international peace and security

treaties: formal agreements among nations that clearly outline their obligations to one another

tribunal: a body appointed to make a judgment

veto: a vote that has the power to block a decision made by others

weapons of mass destruction: weapons designed to kill thousands of people, such as biological, chemical, nuclear, or radiological devices, ranging from poison gas attacks to nuclear explosions

Western nations: the countries of Europe and the Americas

Index

Credits

All of the Internet URLs given in the book were valid at the time of publication. However, due to the dynamic nature of the Internet, some addresses may have changed, or sites may have ceased to exist since publication. While the author and publisher regret any inconvenience this may cause readers, no responsibility for any such changes can be accepted by either the author or the publisher.

Every reasonable effort has been made to trace ownership and to obtain permission to reprint copyright material. The publishers would be pleased to have any errors or omissions brought to their attention so that they may be corrected in subsequent printings.